Strange Elegies

Strange Elegies

Mac Wellman

ROOF BOOKS
NEW YORK

ISBN: 1-931824-16-9
Library of Congress Catalog Card Number: 2005933549

Cover: *The Hundred Black Crows,* Japanese, Edo period, early 17th century
Frontispiece: *The Spider Letter* by Jonathan Edwards

Roof Books are distributed by
Small Press Distribution
1341 Seventh Avenue
Berkeley, CA. 94710-1403.
Phone orders: 800-869-7553
www.spdbooks.org

State of the Arts This book was made possible, in part, with public funds from the
New York State Council on the Arts,
NYSCA a state agency.

Roof Books
are published by
Segue Foundation
303 East 8th Street
New York, NY 10009
segue.org

"... a horseman of indeterminate origins ...
a mysterious rider set against an equally
mysterious background, *l'homme fatal*, in
touch with secret forces, moving in accordance
with occult laws to which all humanity and
indeed all nature is subject ..."
—*Berlin on De Maistre*

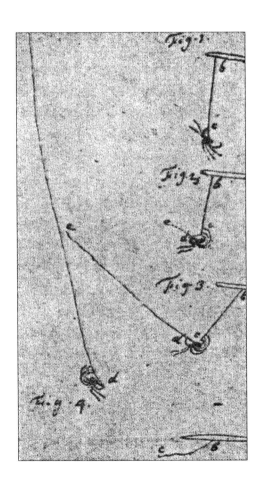

Contents

ELEGY UPON ANY ITEM OF WHICH THE SPEAKER DOES NOT KNOW OR HAS MOMENTARILY FORGOTTEN THE NAME

"Five" for the,
the time
my stand-in
Stood. Re-
boxed
in floral
attributes; it was
Rider's folly

*

The dream of the
thing
thing foretold—as if
quite the
gist of hope's lost—
now all's stable,
the rules writ and
Y.

*

The jurist's deadpan
on the table—
what I'm not
wild about's
Tailed me here:
fatal
bingo. Fatal
fetal
beetle I've forgotten too,

the stem of.
Big bug
with beetle brows.
Ant in the light,
unforgiving . . . . . . O
X upon the
workings of it.

*

Vortex healer;
dot
and re-dot . . .
faulty motor the
so
savaged truth.

*

Bye "Five"
I'd
clear off
of the . . .
Rider's own
how
love to
—o the whiskers'—
Night hates
all—

*

Rider's whole
Ghost
roams of sound.
Falling water in the South
sub-cistern to the

truth
2. Was it *two* or
. . .
?
Maybe the $\sqrt{2}$
aped a
classier
fungible—

*

inexorably yours,
the
naked
truth
skins a knee. Not
to be
an
instance solely—
solo
Rolls over in the
twain. Eye
finds it
cherished
what—
simple word "what". . .

*

the course of it
construed
a mock
mis-step to do
"to do" to
death &
for
what? I...

August in
Japan
maybe, maybe
here or there;
Recall
of waste wadded—
a resistless
assignation of
two's. A swear
ring of no
way to pure measure,
no pain of which—
& what
the me—an
knock of heart's
chromatic. Knack
erred to
bunny. For
the
cat's bad breath . . .
a little lost
black and white kit
shall I? Will
U turn
to the road, idle, wild,
& say there
Stare,
Rider, the
light's out. Ten
tend to
Fall apart with a
whole hand of odd, low hearts . . .

*

So: I'm
not an
item
I know the name of anymore—
; nor dare.
Back
up to here in absence
of there &
"Five"
climbing inside
the porch–
wall, without a
fur of care . . .
& Rider
an "it" now. Ouch!

*

Cast out—
things new.
my
in the wall. For
her. Aches
I'd
Image. Gone
we see
lights of stars put out by
Shape moving over the
hill.

SCAREDY CAT ELEGY

the beautiful thieves
done walked my talk
and so

cause of a chewed tumbler
trouble to remove my hat
follows from the previous
faulty reasoned
nor with a new wrinkle

So: the beanstalk of my allegiances

once the rattle
has wrung

and die young, pathetic. Z
works neat on the down-
side, creeps
whose flag at half-mast?
Whose.
to not know all is enough.

Suborned by theatre
ideologist.

hammering on the inner gong.

child . . .
is a total blank.
Like John Cheese.
Aghast.
Tell. ? why, it
to corn a remote crow.

Quiet . . .
Nor a world of hair.

Of unnecessary givens.
Because
the Grievous hair hook, ripe
for factions'
blooded wheels of
rushes, to
goosed—

Gassed, and ground
Asunder
for it, all gnarly, growls.

*

the tree things go ungathered
while silly death sank.
For the predicate of Pi is
a gorgeous chop clock.

to goe

round

the stanched flow,
thye

the edgeless, unceasing night, the

―――

. . . and suffer no compression
of the world.
Apex, To let the other
slip

Say "Endorphin" to dolphin-gong, that

A Chattahoochie holiday
muscled in upon by robot
hangovers. 0 borax. 0 envelopes.

Rider's real apology.
Time's tooth. But not
Goat. Go and chew on that
ding dong
the sadness of snakes'
whistles in the hot updraft,
in Cenozoic gaps. For
where the low front has teeth
because of not being. Where
as it growls, and glidders.
As it listens to you . . .

and the gown groans out
where

who walks, aimless

in the Land of Evening . . .

and so
Digression finds a low branch
to scratch its hump upon

ELEGY AGAINST THE ARGUMENT FROM DESIGN

Though the nightmare rack
upon it is
not all wet
So: ever, ever, ever.
what rain
wrote it thus—a
simple
goose's

*

My gab has eaten me
up.
River Rider's
wind
doe—lost
to November's
o;
The
night mare of the
three bowls of grub
sprayed with malevolent dust
the cubic
loco=
motive. A summon's
to dream crime:
change
locks and seek
new destiny--
windowless Rider . . .
in & out

*

The logic of design? A
baffle . . .
Be bellows in
heat
to try to be centered
always.
Sniff the
end approaching. Gadzooks!
It is hot. The
0 in know is
snow in July's
omen oven;
Below faith puckers fire.
Truculent tent
& illusion's master . . .
Sink to thy
mission mister
Rider,
kiss it
off—
& sing low

*

nuages & flamelets rip up
the mist road
fabled;
Flower land of door
novelty. To
them
Geese quack true
to know
deceit
reborn as
to be do—
baffle of mob
bright . . .

Rightnesse of bright flower
times the hour
[Rider's time]
to her dread.
I'm wound to a pith,
key-holed.
So: ever, ever, ever.

*

I encounter my fur
I'm flying from.
Furious and were
wolfish. What
irks me
furs me, foldingly
transparent to the poet's weird.
Ravel to riddle
to end king cheese's
domain. Do it
Nope
Star. Go
to floor and hurry
dada;
debouchment. The true linear
horizontal's a
fruitless impact. My
eyes tickle
Rider's
knows . . .
He ruffles his own,
her feathers. Fur
climbs to 31,000 feet and
steady there. Air's
dis advantaged
lingo. A soiled
dream's Rider's

quest.
Shun the South
with its
hub dark and whimsy
of a sea.
The design sells elegance
to aphoristic kids who--
indeed: Who.
?

. . .

WHO ! ?

; so it ever

*

No one will ever read this writ and
up right, for
or against
the algorithm. Cause
of jabber.
Accusation. Defended truths;
The deep entrenchment of design's
all stars'. I'm
climbing out. Ladder down
Scratch my
sore toes &
gird. There is
a place I know not:
Fair the
well: grimmest
Groomboolia; I'm off
to be Rider's own
selfish
Image & gnome.
Only a man jammed
by passion. Fates,

and circumambient
craft. But
Fate's like
fur. Much
hidden. Bend,
shoe
past Design, let her
take me past
love, till love's
more true
than dust or hope.

ELEGY ON FISHHEAD CURRY

. . . taken from an old Malay dream,

Frangipani,
birdpark. Longan,
Rambutan, all,

banana leaf

a world of flats
dangled with
flaps, flapping
laundry;

out here,
we think not.

out here
—*la*—
the tiger in,
the tiger out. There

in Fort Canning Park

consorts with cobras.

true liveliness: fixing
the bicycle while you
are riding upon it.

with six pink
orchids nestled
in a wineglass

the wind-glow glistens-

mid the orchid
sprays, tipping
pajamas the
sarcasm. Futile,
we . . .

Pulau Batam, Ubin:

Red roads gouged
By the giant thumb;

wall the odd Irish
ghost in Raffles' Eld
homestead.

& distant drumrolls
zigzag up the steep
steel empty zone this
tower of a tuning fork
amounts to. Zing . . .

zung.

•

no knowledge inoculates;
OO!
. . .
the better for it,
the true scene inside

so when you go
wish me well.
And square
meaning the Logic

soars, white

so what, you say

in black-letter
black print.

dented lovely. So
pretty she

with *kiasu*
realism. X is
with no comment
with no condescension
with no

forcing mushrooms
up from wet duff,

on a roll. Take out
no

Throw you as it's
thrown me. Clear
off. He brings
disorder's secret
kimono. The hope
that . . .

*

You just stay
there. Agog.
Because all hope
is, is not
say nothing, no.

For the bean pole
person a trifle
abolished,
till Alice from
Atlas be
supposed;
till the so-what wind
rose careless &
if a moth had
marked your
tongue so,

X the Y indeed. For

To smooth
what's wrinkled

till the rotary
nimbus of the
Lord up end
the self, tending to

Day that is
singled out for
X, for

Equal to
equals an

idle jump-rope.

like a wheel
without
a soul.

for turkeys at bay
invoke old hat

deity;
Goose can stay

*

Follow through, to
the end of biography

Bango bengo
Bingo bungo

without a gloss
on possibility's

extract.

Ideas are dime-a-dozen,
unless you don't have

one.

For gho{([o])}ostlier
goes the wormwood,o,
and all X is X
    transposed;

an odd add-on
  up-ends the
    scream. To be

scram

new haircut; same old feathers

For harelip is a
nope

swan.

Cannot catch the flu.

Flue's too
grouchy at saucer
time

Rider's light goes
out. Rider's wit;

bang your head
on the head-board
thing, on the

wigs. Hats. Human hair.

All go scram
at the site of sight,

X serves me, places
time in a tray
before me like hope
like disaster

it tastes pretty much the way it looks

(fish-head curry):

life-like: like life.

ELEGY FOR A WALL EATEN
BY WALL-EATING IVY

Night with rider in its
eases:
ripcord for a tentflap
bollide colossus
ups the ante.
Moon stolen by a whip
rip
for a cap's bill. Stone
saving up a
crazy day.
Rider still assails the

*

Rider grown green with dots
envy the roll
bottom.
7 sails
smile and soon.
Rider whips up and
dust is.
Dust to dust up
and goes off: boom.
Flagged for
an iron
of error, wing and prairie.
frost and stay

*

shuns fear a life, too.
Owls, pop, thimbles,

dart of grasses
frame the, o

*

echo of sleeves, o, o,
constable's
bumpkin fin
flees to open land
lands in a fire, asizzle;
Rider, too, wins wheat
out

*

Out by a cheat's pep,
glimmer of ghost cheese
mimics the sundial.
Grow and go one
Moon dare on a sling
sock.
butter wills to a T-bone, ski
nip and nope.
private antlers fur
the bug joint with
beetle dude.
Behave as if you knew
Wing
what the new is . . .
celebrate rake and
eulogize an apple.
Luck's cake owes you one,
Rider. Rider too
tips the edge till
too . . .
Candle, cat hairs, button, spoon, socks
All stuff out—

*

Way there.
for
myrtle must
a ding dot,
and do.
Who Rider was
dings too. Razzle.

*

View the mess of
all ruined hope,
that true rudder
is gone. Faxed to far
luna. . . . A boiled
Ovoid tells the circuit
verdict. An
egress denied. An
Yew
S
till
it on tune in
Lear-time unwinds, all unweirdy.

Till
it on tune in
Lear-time unwinds, all unweirdy.
Rider is one who fashions amendment
document; who
shapes object, device, a
clover blossom even
;straddles time and time's
out

*

Right angle to the true. So
rights of the riderless
are a
are
an
abridgment, loss of else.
Riders whips a foam of undecidables;
moves along on something else. For the

*

Are a, are an

*

Horseman hath no horse, no below;
Only mystery
landscape, draped in aluminum twists,
sparks, flame, moonish gobo,
phosphor, glow worm's pop.
Walls belie walls. They

*

Creep slow so a

an
inner metallurgic weeps in
hibernation. Fear not, eaten
wall: all's
to be according to Pitter's Pat, Meurt's
bug, Moon's dilemma.
Stuff slows, stinks, blows
away as a
a
a
a dust

doth, done. On a
document of fatal
Candle's out. Rain
torts an upside
water-wall, sheer, of Rider's
Document origin:
Do not trust what the writ
says, says Rider, it is
to be read sideways, sly by
sly, with wet
bugloss, clover, crabgrass, phlox.
Stop to think, why.

*

Rider's tricorn tips to hide.
Sun goes down, somewhere else.
Who's where? Whose
word can redeem the rest? Not
a wall rocking in restless dream, no.
Something has the itchy,
all for tattle. Tatta tatta tatty. The
gun spook
Eerie ere time, spoke.

*

Who tips tricks.
All is to take, all is to not take;
Rider's what wanders
where. Nothing is save the stairs
behind a wall, behind a kitchen
door: darkest caldron, the size–
Spider's mind. A dark bowl
even: We look up, the

West goes slot by slot.
Rider says no to spooks, spooks'
How to, the spooks' not to
Slot.
Spooks and slots and.
So very soon, so very much.
Rider moves along on something else, a
broken trace or
a stake used to brace corner's X in a
snake fence.

Flat on my back, here, the
auld
worm envy,
The
are too
with me, too . . .
task to repair the
& my sorcerer's
cladistics. With
Tom Boyd & Ron Boyd
baptized by
sheer mad shape;
Tiger's wrath is worth
more, too . . .
yet I'll
wear out
the
raptor's heart with a
sky-eyed ribbon
of senseless panoptic view.
Rider's
pyramid
memorializes a new
triptych: you
double U &
who's shoes:
So what's the time
ruined the
with? If it did,
so, unwind connective catgut,
from who's
broken *viola de gumbo*—it
behooves you to

says Rider, at
least; aghast in
error & desire's redoubt,
wicked weaknesses
prick on
cat's folly—
thorn of the
Upon the
no;
no whitenesse, no
matter *how*, how
ideal and thus cherish, tarnish

*

The boat fills with
fierce Bierce
friends [see definition in
Devil] . . .
I'll up too-- maybe,
says who?
says Cynic's
ball-bouncer,
on wit's
empty, he
who did
the
floor cat groom
to get
so with
a soft touch on the
nape, and go
giddy
its
woe. If
black
Dangers wave

at flag. you . . .
Watch them
slowly
rise in amber—
the diametric world of theatre,
hollow to the
heart you know;

*

For at
at that pall that gladdens
you'll not.
Rider refuses
too. A wall
of righteousness holds
to a metric
this who, to
be absolute, if
various and open to the
end of time and
crows' X's
compact with
endedness . . .
So: be dead, be
back alive.
Fatal you,
recall your one true Egret,
stereo in
a cube of floating styrofoam
glazed in slow
day's
a gauze of moonlit . . .
hills
brother
River;

ESTIVAL THORNS

O
here in rust belt
who cares
rebeconung
milwalkety
between that and the
   tangled twine, it
right hand to his left arm
like Poseidon's trumpet,
   a scalloped shelf
of big, dumb feets,

Yeah, them
boots the pooch
dexter and sinister.
I love my Johnny
the way it is.

for fu man crew &
naked coed rugby too

WHO CARES indeed.
Them shits is fly.

This is me.

Ghost was hanging on,
equilibrium a trapeze

It's like a gross
of nested radios. So,
complexier & complexier

(who cares?)
Milwalkety is mind,
is a clinched nail
in the orange, head
of dough, head of head,
head of hedly. Go

blow

Sign "blitz" with a
buzzard catch and

watch (w)hoo a-shiver.
W(hoo)
with her head in ivy. 0
He makes the crazy sign,
for night rats like a thorn
upon my airplane.
Dim. Like a thimble

of swat
a green hill creature
fell out of the truck &
rolled downhill,
a warlock at wit's end.
THE DEVIL KNOWS YOU
REALLY WANT TO.
For what is, to whom,
winds up and wiggles
whistles the wind's tooth—
for the devil is possessed
of perfect skin.
Point is: she swallows
her gun

In the afternoon, she
  rides horse.

Name: Muffy Xcellence.

A thing of mace
rests its case
in the universal
sign of indication.
So turn down the weasel, just
meets the dark glow head-on

rat's noise was truly rabbit;
to half your wit, with an
    engine more
and scout the shout
of probity.

Wemkie! Wemkie!

Is it for this that lumber
begins the hear two acts
screwed down to the refusal
to accept a compliment?

Than the end. The end
is bitter, then
if you could see me you
would most admire

And walked his talk so well
it went a-wishing at the fell
old wishing-well. And so ..

Older now than my brother
or my dad ever got to be,

a suspicious loiterer
talking to no one special
no axe to ask, just

agape and agaze,
sizing up mimbreland—so:

Don't touch my butt in public.

This, too, is a reality;
ability
really;
silly
gilly-flower hour
Surreality. O
value engine
I'm sure
corked. Thorn
is
life-
winged is
spent now.
Is one.
So I'm just a
fare-the-well
sucker
boo!
punched
Hola! Line breaker
Be
bopped. A majestic
man hammertoed
by unclean Fate.
What worms
Waxed.
A Caliban
of rehab. Rahab . . .
CROWS—
normal.
H & G's
clothesline
Georgia: louder

& voiceless
candle
classless S.
Why all the
so casual
in good soup;
L? Voiceless.
L's umbrella
L stop being
breath.

*

Music under the s's.

*

crows' notes useless and a sea of
S's. Affront the
fallen one Rider too

*

X upon the
turtle weave
boats
to bone do. Up on a
twiddle nut
leaves the
broken
too;
belief in smoke crimes.
Jar of acid
bane too
beholden. Chorus.
Me: the saurian rider's
impact song . . .

Ferric. Gnomic
C boat sinks the
in pea sea
canoodle. Do
the,
bright One
"Sky" for Nick the Scaly
Predictable. Who
sells best
delights the wall-eaters . . .
Ride on— super
numerous X, your
eye's an o, a beaten
zero.

With love in vast retreat, on
all sides
O, too true! A
toucan's
wall of woe.

ELEGY UPON AN OLD TAOIST
TEMPLE IN SINGAPORE

turmeric. A newly
devised *longan*
jubilant laundry's
thirty
noble thoughts
nobly express'd.

ivery

peccadillo'd.

Dimension X
with a lawyer
name of Flexie
Zion. True.

bolt of blue . . .

Johore Street's alive
with huge brown
bats, and the usual
conclave of stub-tailed
cats, eyes aglow.

Your toes golden

3 speckled deer
bob in the fen
To round that single source with
massless gluons. A

As if the world before
1965 did not exist.

As the rain thrums
complexity

Silly man said nought;
he silly old man
[Mister Kwang] . . .
so that what
hides, flies in
the face of
and we are winched
with the fullness of
light.

I was too much in a mind

*

What's in the grass
whispers at
in and out. But again
O
. . .
tore the dent was
Y the whole night
long, for X is
darn drag. With a
sense of fictive
wolf written in
Arabic script

and let the wise riddle
the bird wing
long. Let the other
folk

Let no wicked
bicycle

where you are
going is
question asked
so that a sudden
downdraft take
you to
hell

*

Grows a black-heart to be basic
to perfect the zeros'
which was
not cannot

play ball
Hive thinking
frames the core.

So wind the wailing
tinkertoys.
Claw decides.
So would you

Gallops along the
scarlet
shrill
fire-tops as
X the Y, indeed! For
to not do so
hurts the lollard
with old bone
can kicked
a-clank . . .

What is wasted
cannot fear the

Y. To be is to toil
or be tailed
Tapping lightly
on the
equator's hat
to calm the marvelous
seas with the wand

———————————

what is the sky, but
hot air brightened.
So antinoise
the Eupyrion.
To rattle in the weeds
like wind, happy,
with His Majesty
the Sultan of Brunei.

And cinchcraft

   was faire
amidst heather,
   with Boeing

for the rain is a
of light as well
   as water:
in tiny globules
   of cats' eyes

My astrolabe of epithets
gone
done & doth the
visigoth;

wonder did the flightless

bird in.

*

cannot make a
visualization
of ashes.

Rider would
refrain if his
enemies would too;

hide in the chlorine-bin,
then nork the flag

with gust of windiest rhetoric
stilled. Too fog the,
the visionary
diabolo hotel:

a man unconscious
but wide awake.

Speaks to you
most steady
of the Many True
things that are
not;

because the only
error is absence.

I write with ink
never blood.
I never use
recycled paper.

ELEGY on the PROs and CONs
of Renting to Relatives

Amoral Amarillo twitches
uttered in error, a
language of dazzle, delight

and . . .

till the miracle revamps
its look.

forgotten toasts,
forgotten toes . . .

where the land of gradualness
    preens and pops back,
to seek out a new kind of day,
    too hot to handle. My life
when all is hot with black heat,
A clear case of up-ended
    Malvolio.

. . . cause to not say hello
to you know who.

Collision of fact and
factual telling, a

at full-bodied autumnal
satiety

as the worn-out actor
approaches HAMLET.
bored with bread, queerly

at odds
gold wins every time.

a mixture of blood, corn
and it
's golden fleece. The corner
is a fruit of sabat hexes
wriggle-proof, but sexy.

Intense, gasping for a
silver
half-moon of spider's
breath,

because the passage from
heart to
heartless is gradual

because the finite extrudes
from the infinite

like a gaudy boxkite
on fire
on a windless, moonlit
night. Strange
owls bellowing a ritual
owlomniana.

a palindrome.

who guessed correctly
may argue for collapse.

end men's jokes and gags.

Ate the dethsnake like it was
sausage;

Doc Saturday's riposte.
out of spare bicycle parts,
tin cans, scroogies & gorp.

                    . . . I feel bad about the Jawas
          We all feel bad about the Jawas.

Sorta.
As love is made from
anger's rough refract;
a window on ghostly condo
bongo

Surely as the storm's spun
whisper glass out of the
pedestrian frog of fog
flies
; so please respond to us
even if you do not savvy
our computation or cannot
pay the proposed tax due

peccadillo. A fried pillow
buster dusted.
A dry fiddle with the moon in its
mouth.

For Dawn was given
to fishes

*

Doff the minimaximal;
with Pythian Apollo;
bug-lip. Through curtains
of glare

Go to So-So land &
bite

and gasp at the face
of ridicule, rabbit
clobbers the clabber and ups
till there's nothing left
but sonic gradualness

a box of Gordian knots, bics,
spits and you visualize, adrift,
the inhuman *ad hoc*. Go lightly—

drew a golden zigzag
over night's
dark pail;

*

I have swallowtailed the
sword of my own undoing

The crooner coroner
sports a vest and
buries our bones within
a chest of darkest
Mpingo; oh,
drive the door down
the weasel pop.

ELEGY: ON HUMAN HAIR

a single strand of same floating in mid air

On
e
l
o
n
g

|

ofh
a
i
r
on
e
nd
;
l
igh
t
gr
o
w
in
g
(fr
o
mt
h

es
k
ina
o
fm
a
mm
a
ls
;a
p
il
l
iu
s;
a
n
ag
gr
e
ga
t
e

~

o

~

fs
~

uc

~

h
fi
l
li
a
m
e
nt
s,
a
s
th
a
tc
o
ve
r
in
g
th
e
hu
ma
a
nh
e
ad
.

~

)

~

A
s

av
e
r
y
{w
i
se
}
sma
l
la
m
ou
nt,
de
gr
e
e,
m
ea
s
ur
e,
m
ag
n
itu
d
e
,
e
tc.

———

H
air
g

oe
s
o
n
fo
r
ev
e
r
it

|

G
oe
s
fo
e
ve
r
,
so
a
ri
n
g,t
e
a
si
n
gt
h
e
s
le
e

p
in
g
li
p.

*

H
ai
r
is
a
ir
w
i
th
a
n"
H
" i
nf
r
on
t
; (
i
s
d
ea
d
—
c
ut
i
to
f

f?

!

)

~

O

ha

i

r'

t

is

f

ai

r

ex

c

ep

t

wh

e

nf

o

ul

—

O

le

t

th

i

sp

e

r

fe

c

th
a
ir
s
ee
k
am
o
re
p
er
f
ec
t
eq
u
il
i
br
i
um
,
e
ls
e
wh
e
re

:

illustrating the floor.

MACABRE CATFOOD

ALGORIST. ALGOPHOBE. APHORIST
brewed in devils' inkhorn
from thee, sad spider thing
the anecdote of the true
  urn
woo'd. But to still
  endeavor
fly up in furry furies'
buttress. That too sharks
faint noise. You gas up
Thank him for killing them.
The Cheese-Master
  with a mike hidden
cats. Why.
Marks the true representation
with square wheel
made round by wear
dense, with the feel
  of strangeness
Bag the zipper man. A cliff rose
a fuzz. Question is: whose
himself, a pale shadow
  of shimmer
is to what, too. A
Shows.
?
. . .
Goes and tucks that
cheese with tilt.
Behind the green, baggy
  chair ;
too hushed to fragment
  an apostle

though. A titular
hiatus, named Prince
under whose aegis.
To rouse the greenhouse
past a ghost

of cranks & cats. To guess
with no one ready
to bear the truth .

for what gathers the
too. And yet, to hang
    on to the issue
and all there is: joy's
Proud Republic. Say no
greensleeves with feather.

Ne'er-do-wells, the
    unenlightenable
wicket-twisters, those
with intense, local thoughts
    hung out to dry.

Calloo! Callayl Callumbus ...
Skews what Rider knew.
The bearer of the this message,

Take it up
Nuncle, nuncle, what bad
resembles the crooked hoof
For what the snake
opines holds true
of one not like you, who
into that good bite.
I find finally what's inside
you go, wasting someone
    else's time.

with knowing what to
   say.
Another day without.
And snow goes slow to back.
Crystal
cases it, brilliant on the road
Sizzling.

MEPHITIC BUGLES

YOUR HAT IN FLAMES OF ORANGE, YOU
  utter the word
hoarse, with the cry of
  new life, o, o,
which rivers it out. A
unswerving corn. The shrill
noise of night, and blankest
bottomless despair,
so that what never was, is.
My life reminds me
of my life.
No message on the radio
  hurts; no
relishes at wishbone's shot
when the ghost cries in the
chimney.

The day arrives when nothing
further to be said collides
with tinny evenness. What gases
blank, with a crick in the back.
0, resolves in inky
anti-glide. What can tax
taxies an alien taxonomy.
To crie out in silly pageantry,
all men

because New York City
wants you to. You hear
new things, things
spoken in a new way.
Go, and speckle the thrushes'
nape; go and ribbon the

rainbow trout. Night
of four dreams, one
of them real. One of them
round as

the key word is "random",
randomly misused. Gear
up and out.
White crow,
black crow
and finger paint.
The man who wrote "boat"
and believed it
in a fog of semi-lucid
penumbra.
Sands of Iwo-Jimaish. Yes,
bustle my hut.
High and low, the glow boxes'
escape vitrified the pale
Januarian stubble. Escape
escapes, preens exchanging
hot leather for a wicked
thorn.

So to flash, in pain, a
thing of wing shut
dilapido! Up to and
zat's

no case of tragic shirt-tails;

duck a do;
and her nest
of cacophonous
eumenides—
battered hill tribe
seeks rondo rebound;

a classic shinerizes
some indeed chew.
Draw clear of claw.
If no account duckweed
till there's nothing
left.

. . . and icy forks and moons
And perpendicular

Ballyhoo. Along
the wilted avenues
of desire a
turk of rats, man.

Give to what gloss
causes to spit.
And, yea, the wreck is
wrack; and black as crow,
or clarinet's mpingo.
Till we sing and spray
like tipsy marionettes
of Marinette *bwa chech*—
"terrible" Marinette—
"of the dry arms".

Wacko dumbbell drive
doctors
dollars out of cheese.
O! O!
Fall silent now.

ELVIS ON THE MOON

ABORIGINES HAVE TRANSPORTED DAD
THROUGH TIME.
Tumble, toil and
don't bottom the lock
for an anti systematic argument,
an

despite the gloomy Atrides.

chute.
They walk like the
moon's golden stalk, on
a roundabout. You stream,
they bite their own cladistics,

quadrille. With scalloped
ears, a flaming guitar, a
rock, the

Yet what comes after
rotates in pure Gas.
Ask no captious owl.
Swedish. Like shoe polish
alien sharks.

Make way for the big
Wiggle bump.

A club geeks no grub nor
a jinxed thing on thongs—
what wish did to boo
the bone frill

Great woe bleeds through
warlock's place. A topic
Before the hurry-up faded
ruby. The gemstone
   salaam

hang feet by charade
   door

and hope
and while what walks not
crept

whose shoes has been waxed
and Y. For there is]ust not
enough aire to be wholly
sectioned by a mere emotion.

It's grey fact for being, all
to its nadir, a continuum.
Singular algorithm. That
Spider of hope, threading
on display for proper
   derelicts and

the paranoid parousia of a

second-grade second coming:

Ends up a canned voice.
A *karaoke* cowboy. No one,
but Rider could so

when what cools, rankles
with an itch, too.

Protect me from surges

glazed in emerald. And old
to not black out;

runs amok with foreign sauces
Feet have need of elbows
too;
under the stern Mesozoic
salto mortale

All care to the windy
coast cost
is banished by thought's bone,

Round the hard, chill
charred hill of change,
from under my feet. Just
the fur hears the bare fly.

A furry turns to asphodel . . .

ROOF BOOKS

- ❏ Andrews, Bruce. **EX WHY ZEE**. 112p. $10.95.
- ❏ Andrews, Bruce. **Getting Ready To Have Been Frightened**. 116p. $7.50.
- ❏ Benson, Steve. **Blue Book**. Copub. with The Figures. 250p. $12.50
- ❏ Bernstein, Charles. **Controlling Interests**. 80p. $11.95.
- ❏ Bernstein, Charles. **Islets/Irritations**. 112p. $9.95.
- ❏ Bernstein, Charles (editor). **The Politics of Poetic Form**.
  246p. $12.95; cloth $21.95.
- ❏ Brossard, Nicole. **Picture Theory**. 188p. $11.95.
- ❏ Cadiot, Olivier. **Former, Future, Fugitive**. Translated by Cole Swensen.
  166p. $13.95.
- ❏ Champion, Miles. **Three Bell Zero**. 72p. $10.95.
- ❏ Child, Abigail. **Scatter Matrix**. 79p. $9.95.
- ❏ Davies, Alan. **Active 24 Hours**. 100p. $5.
- ❏ Davies, Alan. **Signage**. 184p. $11.
- ❏ Davies, Alan. **Rave**. 64p. $7.95.
- ❏ Day, Jean. **A Young Recruit**. 58p. $6.
- ❏ Di Palma, Ray. **Motion of the Cypher**. 112p. $10.95.
- ❏ Di Palma, Ray. **Raik**. 100p. $9.95.
- ❏ Doris, Stacy. **Kildare**. 104p. $9.95.
- ❏ Dreyer, Lynne. **The White Museum**. 80p. $6.
- ❏ Dworkin, Craig. **Strand**. 112p. $12.95.
- ❏ Edwards, Ken. **Good Science**. 80p. $9.95.
- ❏ Eigner, Larry. **Areas Lights Heights**. 182p. $12, $22 (cloth).
- ❏ Gizzi, Michael. **Continental Harmonies**. 92p. $8.95.
- ❏ Gladman, Renee. **A Picture-Feeling**. 72p. $10.95.
- ❏ Goldman, Judith. **Vocoder**. 96p. $11.95.
- ❏ Gottlieb, Michael. **Ninety-Six Tears**. 88p. $5.
- ❏ Gottlieb, Michael. **Gorgeous Plunge**. 96p. $11.95.
- ❏ Gottlieb, Michael. **Lost & Found**. 80p. $11.95.
- ❏ Greenwald, Ted. **Jumping the Line**. 120p. $12.95.
- ❏ Grenier, Robert. **A Day at the Beach**. 80p. $6.
- ❏ Grosman, Ernesto. **The XULReader: An Anthology of Argentine Poetry
  (1981–1996)**. 167p. $14.95.
- ❏ Guest, Barbara. **Dürer in the Window, Reflexions on Art**.
  Book design by Richard Tuttle. Four color throughout. 80p. $24.95.
- ❏ Hills, Henry. **Making Money**. 72p. $7.50. VHS videotape $24.95.
  Book & tape $29.95.
- ❏ Huang Yunte. **SHI: A Radical Reading of Chinese Poetry**. 76p. $9.95
- ❏ Hunt, Erica. **Local History**. 80 p. $9.95.
- ❏ Kuszai, Joel (editor) **poetics@**, 192 p. $13.95.

- ❏ Inman, P. **Criss Cross**. 64 p. $7.95.
- ❏ Inman, P. **Red Shift**. 64p. $6.
- ❏ Lazer, Hank. **Doublespace**. 192 p. $12.
- ❏ Levy, Andrew. **Paper Head Last Lyrics**. 112 p. $11.95.
- ❏ Mac Low, Jackson. **Representative Works: 1938–1985**. 360p. $18.95 (cloth).
- ❏ Mac Low, Jackson. **Twenties**. 112p. $8.95.
- ❏ McMorris, Mark. **The Café at Light**. 112p. $12.95.
- ❏ Moriarty, Laura. **Rondeaux**. 107p. $8.
- ❏ Neilson, Melanie. **Civil Noir**. 96p. $8.95.
- ❏ Osman, Jena. **An Essay in Asterisks**. 112p. $12.95.
- ❏ Pearson, Ted. **Planetary Gear**. 72p. $8.95.
- ❏ Perelman, Bob. **Virtual Reality**. 80p. $9.95.
- ❏ Perelman, Bob. **The Future of Memory**. 120p. $14.95.
- ❏ Piombino, Nick, **The Boundary of Blur**. 128p. $13.95.
- ❏ Prize Budget for Boys, **The Spectacular Vernacular Revuew**. 96p. $14.95.
- ❏ Raworth, Tom. **Clean & Will-Lit**. 106p. $10.95.
- ❏ Robinson, Kit. **Balance Sheet**. 112p. $11.95.
- ❏ Robinson, Kit. **Democracy Boulevard**. 104p. $9.95.
- ❏ Robinson, Kit. **Ice Cubes**. 96p. $6.
- ❏ Scalapino, Leslie. **Objects in the Terrifying Tense Longing from Taking Place**. 88p. $9.95.
- ❏ Seaton, Peter. **The Son Master**. 64p. $5.
- ❏ Sherry, James. **Popular Fiction**. 84p. $6.
- ❏ Silliman, Ron. **The New Sentence**. 200p. $10.
- ❏ Silliman, Ron. **N/O**. 112p. $10.95.
- ❏ Smith, Rod. **Music or Honesty**. 96p. $12.95
- ❏ Smith, Rod. **Protective Immediacy**. 96p. $9.95
- ❏ Stefans, Brian Kim. **Free Space Comix**. 96p. $9.95
- ❏ Tarkos, Christophe. **Ma Langue est Poétique—Selected Works**. 96p. $12.95.
- ❏ Templeton, Fiona. **Cells of Release**. 128p. with photographs. $13.95.
- ❏ Templeton, Fiona. **YOU—The City**. 150p. $11.95.
- ❏ Torres, Edwin. **The All-Union Day of the Shock Worker**. 112 p. $10.95.
- ❏ Tysh, Chris. **Cleavage**. 96p. $11.95.
- ❏ Ward, Diane. **Human Ceiling**. 80p. $8.95.
- ❏ Ward, Diane. **Relation**. 64p. $7.50.
- ❏ Watson, Craig. **Free Will**. 80p. $9.95.
- ❏ Watten, Barrett. **Progress**. 122p. $7.50.
- ❏ Weiner, Hannah. **We Speak Silent**. 76 p. $9.95
- ❏ Weiner, Hannah. **Page**. 136 p. $12.95
- ❏ Wolsak, Lissa. **Pen Chants**. 80p. $9.95.
- ❏ Yasusada, Araki. **Doubled Flowering: From the Notebooks of Araki Yasusada**. 272p. $14.95.

ROOF BOOKS
are published by
Segue Foundation
300 Bowery
New York, NY 10012
Visit our website at **segue.org**

ROOF BOOKS are distributed by
SMALL PRESS DISTRIBUTION
1341 Seventh Avenue
Berkeley, CA. 94710-1403.
Phone orders: 800-869-7553
spdbooks.org